GO FOR IT!™

BASKETBALL

FOR BOYS AND GIRLS

START RIGHT AND PLAY WELL

by Bill Gutman

with Illustrations
by Ben Brown

MARSHALL CAVENDISH
CORPORATION

GREY CASTLE PRESS

Marshall Cavendish Edition, Freeport, New York.

Published by arrangement with Grey Castle Press, Lakeville, Ct.

Printed in the USA

The Library of Congress Cataloging in Publication Data

Gutman, Bill.
    Basketball : start right and play well / by Bill Gutman ; with illustrations by Ben Brown.
        p.   cm. — (Go for it!)
   Summary: Describes the history and current teams, leagues, and championships of basketball and provides instruction on how to play the game.
   ISBN 0-942545-92-3 (lib. bdg.)
   1. Basketball—Juvenile literature. [1. Basketball.] I. Brown, Ben, 1921–   Ill. II. Title. III. Series: Gutman, Bill. Go for it!
GV885.1.G87   1990
796.323—dc20
                              89-7606
                              CIP
                              AC

Photo credits: Focus On Sports, page 8, bottom; UPI/Bettmann Newsphotos, page 8, top.

Special thanks to: Ernie Zafonte, varsity basketball coach, Dover Junior/Senior High School, Dover Plains, N.Y.

Picture research: Omni Photo Communications, Inc.

ABOUT THE AUTHOR

Bill Gutman is the author of over 70 books for children and young adults. The majority of his titles have dealt with sports, in both fiction and non-fiction, including "how-to" books. His name is well-known to librarians who make it their business to be informed about books of special interest to boys and reluctant readers. He lives in Poughquag, New York.

ABOUT THE ILLUSTRATOR

Ben Brown's experience ranges from cartoonist to gallery painter. He is a graduate of the High School of Music & Art in New York City and the University of Iowa Art School. He has been a member of the National Academy of Design and the Art Students' League. He has illustrated government training manuals for the disadvantaged (using sports as themes), and his animation work for the American Bible Society won two blue ribbons from the American Film Festival. He lives in Great Barrington, Massachusetts.

In order to keep the instructions in this book as simple as possible, the author has chosen in most cases to use "he" to signify both boys and girls.

A BRIEF HISTORY

Basketball may be the only major sport that was actually invented by request. It happened when one man asked another to create a new sport that could be played indoors during the winter months.

The place was Springfield, Massachusetts, and the year was 1891. Dr. Luther Gulick was the head of the physical training department of the International Training School of the Young Men's Christian Association. The same school would later become Springfield College. But in the winter of 1891, Dr. Gulick was worried.

He felt that the young men at the school were tired of the same winter activities—calisthenics, drills, and throwing a medicine ball around. So Dr. Gulick went to another teacher at the school, 29-year-old James Naismith. He told Naismith that the boys at the school needed something new and exciting to do. He asked the younger man to try to devise a new game.

Naismith thought about it for several weeks. Slowly, the idea for the new game began to take place. Naismith knew he wanted to use a large, light ball that could be handled with the hands. Because the game was to be played indoors, he didn't want any running with the ball. That would get too rough.

In addition, the young teacher wanted very little physical contact. He also felt there should be a goal into which the ball should be thrown. And he decided it should be above the floor.

From those feelings came the new sport. Some people wanted to call it "Naismith-ball." But the game's inventor decided a better name was "basketball."

The first hoops were old wooden peach baskets nailed to the balcony of the gymnasium. There were nine men on a side for the first game and just one basket was scored. Despite this, the boys at Springfield liked the new game and continued to play. Pretty soon, it was spreading to other YMCA's in the area.

In the early days, the rules were never the same in any two places. At Cornell, they once tried to play the game with 25 players on a side. Others played it outdoors, with a basket simply suspended at the top of a pole. But it wasn't long before the colleges began playing the new game and some of the modern rules came into effect.

The ball was always put into play by a center jump. In 1893, the five-man game was played in smaller gyms. By 1897, the free-throw line was moved to 15 feet from the basket, where it remains today. That same year the five-man game became the standard.

Many colleges were playing the sport before the turn of the century. And it wasn't long afterward that barnstorming professional teams appeared. The pros had a rough life then. They would travel from town to town, playing in all kinds of halls and gyms for just a few dollars a game. They often played on courts surrounded by a wire net or steel cage. In the net-and-cage games, the ball was always in play, and that play sometimes got very rough.

One of the great early professional teams was the Original Celtics. Some of the stars of that ballclub were Nat Holman, Chris Leonard, Dutch Dehnert, Pete Barry, Johnny Beckman, and Joe Lapchick. Other early teams were Eddie Gottlieb's Philadelphia SPHAs, the Troy (New York) Trojans and two black teams, the New York Renaissance and Harlem Globetrotters.

But again, there were few pro leagues. Those that did start, quickly folded. But the college game continued to grow. Great rivalries began to develop. Most of the players were small back then. The basket was 10-feet high, as it is today, and none of the players made the spectacular kind of slam dunks seen in today's game.

Yet by the 1930s, fans were jamming New York's Madison Square Garden to watch top college doubleheaders. In 1939, the first NCAA post-season tournament was held. Also, the National Invitational Tournament (NIT) had been created to follow the regular season. The two tournaments helped the game to grow even faster.

By the middle 1940s, basketball had its first two real giants. They were 6-foot, 10-inch George Mikan at DePaul University, and 7-foot Bob "Foothills" Kurland at Oklahoma A & M. Both Mikan and Kurland worked hard to become top all-around players. They proved that very tall men could also be great athletes.

The National Basketball Association got started in the late 1940s. By the middle 1950s, basketball fans were cheering the likes of Mikan, Bob Cousy, Dolph Schayes, Paul Arizin, Bob Pettit, George Yardley, Jack Twyman and other fine players. Within a few short years, they would be joined by Bill Russell, Wilt Chamberlain, Elgin Baylor, Oscar Robertson, Rick Barry, Jerry West, Jerry Lucas, John Havlicek and others greats who helped bring the pro game into the modern age.

In the NBA, players like Julius "Doctor J" Erving, Kareem Abdul Jabbar, Larry Bird, Earvin "Magic" Johnson and Michael "Air" Jordan have thrilled crowds with some of the greatest basketball ever seen.

Today, basketball has become a worldwide game. There are

One of the great individual battles of the 1960s featured center Wilt Chamberlain (left) of Philadelphia and Bill Russell (6) of Boston. Both National Basketball Association superstars were great players in their own right and would be voted into the Basketball Hall of Fame.

Earvin "Magic" Johnson has changed the face of basketball by showing that a 6-9 player could play point guard. Johnson handles the ball as well as any small man. He is a great passer and floor leader. But he can also go inside and rebound with the big guys.

professional leagues in Spain, Italy, Israel and other countries. Teams from the Soviet Union, Brazil, Puerto Rico and Canada have all done well in the Olympic Games and other amateur tournaments. Many American players now play in other countries.

Women's basketball has also grown in recent years. Although women played almost as early the men, the women's game did not really develop. For years, the rules were different and the game hardly looked like real basketball. But the rules slowly changed to make the women's game more like the men's.

Then in 1972, Congress passed an amendment to the Civil Rights Act of 1964 that made colleges and universities offer the same programs to women as to men, including sports. From that point on, women's basketball developed into a fast-paced game. Players like Carol Blazejowski, Nancy Lieberman, Lynette Woodard, Ann Meyers, Cheryl Miller and Sue Wicks are just some of the great women players of the past 15 years.

Basketball has come a long way since James Naismith first hooked up a pair of peach baskets. It has become a major sport and an international game. Today's players are great athletes who electrify crowds everywhere. The game is bigger and better than ever, and still growing.

ORGANIZED
BASKETBALL

The National Basketball Association is the major league of basketball. In the 1988–89 season, the league expanded to 25 teams. Salaries are also higher than ever, with the top players making two million dollars a year or more.

As mentioned before, there are also pro leagues in other countries, as well as a Continental League in the eastern United States. Some of the foreign leagues pay a great deal of money for good American players. The Continental League pays less. It is almost like a minor league. Most players in the other leagues dream of playing in the NBA.

The National Collegiate Athletic Association (NCAA) is the governing body for college basketball. There are programs at almost every college and university, large and small. Each plays a schedule in its own division against schools of similar size. And the ballplayers keep getting better all the time.

But that's because basketball is everywhere. There are hoops in many driveways and backyards all around the land. Every playground and gymnasium has a basketball court. The game is played in both cities and rural areas. And there are leagues at every level. Young people can begin playing organized basketball as soon as they reach school, where there are intramural and other organized programs. High school basketball is a popular winter sport everywhere, just as James Naismith wanted it to be.

The Game Of Basketball

Basketball is played on a court that measures 94 feet long by 50 feet wide, though some courts are smaller. With players getting bigger, faster and stronger through the years, there has been talk of making the court even larger. But this has never been done.

The game, of course, is played with five players to a side. The object is to put a leather ball, which is from 29½ inches to 30¼ inches in circumference, through a round metal circle, or goal. The goal, or basket, is 18 inches in diameter. There is a mesh net attached to the rim, open at the bottom so the ball can drop through.

Players advance the ball toward the goal by passing or bouncing it. Bouncing is called "dribbling." A player cannot take more than one step without dribbling the ball. Otherwise, he is "traveling." That is a violation and his team loses the ball.

A basket, or field goal, counts two points. However, in recent years, high school, college and pro ball have allowed a three-point field goal on long shots from behind a special line on the court. Free throws count just one point.

The regulation basketball court has had the same basic dimensions for many years. The only change brought about by bigger players has been the free throw lane. It used to be only six feet across. Today in high school and college, it is 12 feet wide, and in the professional game it is 16 feet wide.

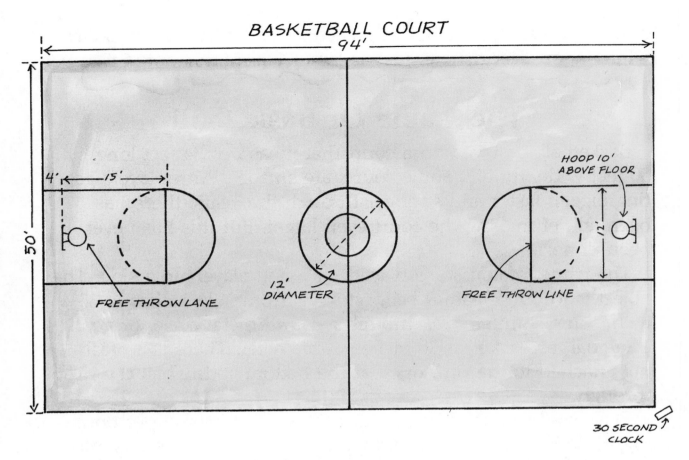

BASKETBALL COURT

A standard basketball is made of leather and is from 29½ to 30¼ inches in circumference.

The free-throw line is 15 feet from the basket, which is 10 feet off the floor. The hoop, or rim, is mounted to a rectangular backboard, made of wood, fiber glass, clear Plexiglas or other materials. The backboard is four feet high and six feet wide. The rim is mounted in the middle of the board, 18 inches from the bottom. The front of the rim extends four feet out from the end line of the court.

Shots at the basket can be taken from anywhere on the court. But it is always easier to make a shot near the basket than one from far out. So a team offense usually tries to work the ball inside. If they can't do that, they try to get a man open, so he can shoot without a defender near him.

Defenders, of course, try to intercept passes or steal the ball from a dribbler. But they cannot make body contact while doing it. A missed shot is up for grabs. Both teams can try for the rebound. If the defensive team gets it, they then go on offense and move the ball toward their opponent's goal. If the offense gets the rebound, they can put the ball right back up into the basket. Or if that isn't possible, they can throw it back outside and start the offense over again.

Defensive players are allowed to block shots as they are taken. But a man blocking or trying to block a shot cannot make contact with the offensive player. If he slaps him on his shooting hand or arm, or hits him with his body, a foul will be called. Also, a player cannot block a shot that is already headed downward toward the basket. If he does, "goal tending" is called. Though the ball doesn't go through the basket, the team and player who took the shot get credit for the hoop.

In high school and college basketball, a player committing five personal fouls must leave the game. In the pros, it takes six fouls before a player must leave. That is called "fouling out."

In pro ball, a team has just 24 seconds to get a shot off. In the college game, several "shot-clock" rules have been tried in recent years. Now a 45-second clock is used. High school girls use a 30-second clock, though the boys in most regions don't have a shot clock. The rules still vary a bit on this detail of the game.

Game times also become longer as the age of the players increases. High school games consist of four, eight-minute quarters for a 32-minute game. College games last 40 minutes, with two, 20-minute halves. The pros play a 48-minute game, broken into four, 12-minute quarters. If a game is tied at the end, teams must play a short overtime. In fact, they must play as many overtimes as are necessary to have a winner. There can be no ties in basketball. Overtimes are five minutes long in the pros and college, three minutes in high school ball.

Coaches can send substitutes into the game at the end of a period, during time outs, or during a stop in the action for a foul or violation. There are generally two officials "working" a basketball game. They call the fouls and violations. If a player or coach argues a foul call or displays unsportsmanlike conduct, a

On a jump ball, the referee will toss the ball in the air between two opposing players. Each player must be poised to jump as soon as the ball leaves the ref's hand. It is important that a player time his leap so he is at the top of his jump as soon as the ball falls back within reach.

technical foul may be called. This means a member of the other team gets a free shot. Whether he makes it or not, his team gets the ball back.

Normally, the ball changes hands after a basket, a successful free throw or a violation. The other team passes it in from out of bounds. But the defensive team can try to intercept the pass.

Games are started by a jump ball, or center jump. Two players line up in the circle at mid-court and the referee throws the ball up in between them. They both leap and try to tap it to a teammate to start play.

Basketball today is a fast-paced, exciting game. Today's players are fine athletes who can handle the ball like magicians. They can dribble behind their backs and between their legs. They can take jump shots from long range, and many can slam dunk from in close. Yet these same players can also be great on defense, so the scores aren't always out of sight.

A tough defense always tries to disrupt the offense. When there is a loose ball, every player nearby must try to get it. This often leads to bumping and diving, with players sometimes winding up on the floor.

The Positions

There are several basic positions on a basketball team. Where you play may be decided by your size and the individual skills you have. The players who usually handle the ball the most are the two *guards*. They are generally smaller and quicker than the others and have the job of bringing the ball up the court and setting up the offense.

A guard must dribble and pass well, and should be able to shoot from the outside. He must also be able to drive hard to the basket if there is an opening.

Forwards usually play in the forecourt or up front. They move back and forth along the baseline and sometimes come out to the side of the foul circle. They rarely come all the way out behind the key. Forwards have to be good shooters from the corners or sides, and must be able to go underneath the boards and rebound. They should also be able to pass well. And while they might not have to dribble as well as a guard, they should have the basic skill.

The *center* is usually the tallest player on the team. He plays in the middle on offense, or "in the pivot," as it used to be called. The center must have good hands to receive all kinds of passes from his guards and forwards. He must also be able to pass well, to hit players cutting down the middle or past him. And he should be able to make a short jump shot and maybe even a hook shot from in close.

As a rule, the center doesn't need the shooting range of a guard or forward. And he usually doesn't have to dribble the ball much. But he must be a good rebounder and tough underneath the boards. If a center is a very skilled player, chances are that both the offense and defense will revolve around him. If he has limited skills, the coach will then use him as part of an overall team concept.

Young players should really play all the positions. By doing that, they will get a better understanding of the game. They will know what is expected of guards, forwards, and a center on both offense and defense. This will help them become complete players.

If your coach makes you a forward or center, don't think you can go easy on some of the skills used by a guard. Players today must be able to do everything. It doesn't matter how tall or short they are or where they play. The game is so highly skilled that big guys can dribble and little guys can rebound. And that's the way it should be.

Getting Ready To Play

To play basketball well, you've got to be in top physical condition. There is no way around this. Basketball is a game of running and jumping, of speed and quickness, of switching instantly from offense to defense. Players sometimes have to go at full speed for many minutes on end.

So if you plan to play the game, you must realize there is much more to basketball than just shooting. You've got to get yourself ready even before the season starts. How do you do it?

Everyone should begin by running. Basketball is a game of endurance and stamina, along with the individual skills. A tired player cannot perform well. And a tired team is going to be run right off the court. So every young player must begin by getting himself in running condition.

This is done in two ways. One is to set up a regular running or jogging schedule. Distance running of at least several miles

One of the best exercises a young basketball player can do is to jump rope. It not only helps a player to increase stamina and endurance, but it helps with jumping ability and coordination as well.

three times a week will help build stamina and staying power. But this type of training must also be combined with stop-and-start sprinting.

Wind sprints of perhaps 20 or 30 yards are a good idea. Sprint as hard as you can one way, stop, turn, then sprint back. In fact, you can sometimes shorten the distance and maybe sprint for ten yards, then stop, then go 15. This way, you will be varying the distances that you have to run hard, just as you will in a game.

Once you begin to get into good shape, you can combine your workouts with a kind of interval training. During your long distance run, suddenly sprint all out for maybe 15 or 20 yards, then go right back to the jogging pace. If you do this a number of times during your run, it will strengthen and toughen you even more. Also, it will condition your leg muscles to the kind of stop-and-start running you need in basketball.

In addition to running, a young player should do some drills to improve coordination. Jumping rope is an especially good exercise. It will not only improve an athlete's coordination, but will also get him used to the constant jumping the sport requires. Like running, it will improve endurance and stamina as well.

Another good preseason workout involves moving from side to side and even backwards. There will be times during a game when you will have to backpedal quickly, or run from one side of the court to the other. As a rule, this movement should be made with short, quick strides, which make it easier to stop and change direction.

Young players can then practice quick, side-to-side movements. They can do this by "sliding" to the side. In other words, not crossing one leg in front of the other. There are also times when the movement will involve the crossover step. Both of these should be practiced for quickness and coordination. The same with the backpedaling movement. Once again, short, but quick steps are the best way.

Before any kind of workout—whether jogging, sprinting or jumping rope—young players should be sure to warm up. Stretching the muscles is all important. There are a number of basic exercises that can be done. Toe touching is one. Spread your feet comfortably apart and keep your knees straight. Then bend and touch each hand to the opposite toe. Do it slowly and hold the position.

Putting one leg up on a rail or a chair back and sliding both hands toward your foot is another good warm up to stretch the legs, especially the hamstrings. As with all stretching, do the exercise slowly and hold the final position for five or ten seconds. Repeat each exercise at least five times.

Legs, back and stomach muscles can be stretched by lying on your back and bringing both legs straight up over your head until they touch the ground behind you. Hold and lower them slowly. After this is done, you can also raise each thigh back toward your chest, pulling on the leg with both hands to stretch the muscles even more. This, too, is done lying down, one leg at a time.

There are other exercises that can also be done. Perhaps you already know some, or your coach might have some ideas. But stretching before and after a workout is important for a basketball player. Muscles must be loose and flexible at all times.

It isn't necessary for every ballplayer to be super strong. But good strength can only help out on the court, especially under the boards, where there is always a lot of shoving and banging. So young players should be conscious of their strength.

In most cases, natural exercises are the best. Young players can easily do pushups and perhaps pullups to strengthen arms and shoulders. Girls, too, can do modified or regular pushups. Working with a commercial hand grip or just squeezing a rubber ball will also help strengthen hands and forearms.

Weight training is another story. Basketball players are urged to use weights very carefully. Flexibility is important in developing shooting ability. Therefore a young player doesn't want to tie up his muscles through the wrong kind of weight training. If you want to use weights, get some advice from a coach.

As a rule, use lower weights and simply repeat the exercise

more times. And always make sure to keep up with your stretching. If there is any sign of your arms, shoulders or back tightening up, then it might be best to stop.

Good conditioning also means good everyday living habits. That means balancing your daily schedule. You've got to leave time for practice, but still do your schoolwork and any chores you might have around the house. Because you're playing a sport that takes a great deal of energy, you must always be sure to get enough rest.

It's also important to eat well during an action-packed, busy season. That means a well-balanced diet with lots of fresh fruits and vegetables, healthy snacks, and plenty of water and juices. Avoid too much junk food, fried and greasy foods, and sugary snacks. Needless to say, alcohol, tobacco and drugs will ruin your chances for a successful season.

Equipment

There really isn't much equipment needed to play basketball. Shorts and a jersey are the only uniform you'll need, and sometimes your team will supply that. Boys, of course, should always wear an athletic supporter. Both boys and girls will also need socks and maybe a sweatband to wear around their foreheads.

The most important piece of equipment a basketball player needs are his shoes. An ill-fitting or uncomfortable pair of sneakers can go a long way toward ruining your game. So every player must take real care in picking out a pair of game shoes.

Today, an inexpensive pair of sneakers may cost just ten or fifteen dollars. But the better shoes might cost thirty five to forty dollars, or even more. A general rule is to get the best quality sneakers you can afford. After all, the running, stopping, cutting and jumping are not easy on the feet.

There are both high top and low-cut style sneakers. Neither is better than the other. It all depends on what feels most comfortable to you. Most basketball shoes have small ridges running parallel across the soles to grab the wooden courts in gymnasiums. Some others have small raised circles on the bottoms. Make sure the soles are right and that you are buying a basketball shoe.

It's been said that while leather shoes give the best support, canvas and nylon shoes will wear better. Nylon shoes "breathe" on the feet and will dry out faster when they get soaked with perspiration. So the type of shoe is another decision you will have to make.

Also, when you are trying a shoe on, make sure you are wearing the same kind of socks you wear on the court. In other words, if you wear two pairs of socks during practice and games, wear two pairs when you try on your sneakers. Even with two pairs of socks, you should leave at least a quarter inch of room in the toe. Feet can swell slightly during a fast-paced game.

It might also be wise to use one pair of sneakers for indoor playing, and another pair for outdoors. A cement or asphalt court will chew up the bottoms of sneakers much faster than a wood gym floor. That doesn't mean to use a pair of worn-out, tattered sneakers outdoors. You still need good support for the pounding your feet will take.

So take care when buying your basketball shoes. Of course, they won't automatically make you a better player. But good shoes will make it easier for you to become a better player.

LEARNING TO PLAY BASKETBALL

Dribbling

Dribbling or bouncing the basketball has been an important skill ever since the beginning of the game. Today, every player on a team must be able to "put the ball on the floor." That means to dribble. In today's game, it means to be able to handle the ball with both hands. In fact, the skill should be almost automatic. The player should not have to look at the ball as he bounces it. He should be able to change hands quickly, as well as go behind his back and between his legs if he has to.

Yet this is not a skill that comes easily. To become a good ball handler takes a great deal of practice. There are many ways a new player can practice on his own. But he also has to be able to use the skill under game conditions, with a defensive player breathing down his back.

The first basic rule of dribbling is to keep the ball low. The ball should never bounce higher than your waist. In fact, when dribbling in heavy traffic, you can also get low, bending forward from the waist and at the knees. A lower center of gravity gives you more control of the ball and makes it more difficult for a defender to steal it.

When dribbling, keep your fingers spread. The tips of the fingers control the ball. As the ball comes up off the floor, you should meet it with your hand, giving slightly as the ball hits. Within a split second, the fingers push the ball back toward the floor.

Left. Every basketball player today should be able to dribble the ball well with both hands without really looking at it. This takes many hours of practice. One good drill is to blindfold yourself and practice handling the ball without looking. Pretty soon the ball will begin to feel as if it's part of your hand and arm.
Right. Another good dribbling drill for the beginner is to practice while kneeling. Bouncing the ball a shorter distance to the floor will help the young player to get the feel of the ball with both hands. The player can also get used to the pumping, dribbling motion of the arm and hand.

The forearm, from the elbow to fingertips, will move in a kind of pumping action during the basic bouncing of the ball. A young player learning to dribble should repeat this motion with both hands, simply bouncing the ball up and down. Before long, he will find himself bouncing it without looking. At that point, the dribble will begin to feel natural.

But that's only step one. Once you feel comfortable bouncing the ball, you must begin to move with it. Do this by bouncing the ball slightly in front of yourself, walking as you do so. This walking drill can be practiced in all directions. Begin walking forward, then backward, then to the right and left. While you are dribbling at this slow place, look down at the ball as little as possible. Feel it, as if it is part of your arm and hand. This is perhaps the most important advice for successful ballhandling.

The next step is to speed everything up. Begin moving faster

Once a ballhandler has confidence, he will be able to dribble hard with either hand. He won't have to watch his dribble and can keep his eyes on the court in front of him. He will also be able to change hands and directions without hesitation. And then he'll really be helping his team.

with the ball. You will keep picking up the pace until you can run full speed while still dribbling. At that point, you can do your wind sprints with the basketball. Now you can do two things at once.

Once you have mastered the basics of dribbling with both hands, then you can really begin to improve. But it will take a great deal of work. The good dribbler can switch the ball from one hand to the other in the blink of an eye. He can do this while moving at full speed by simply bouncing the ball across the front of his body and receiving it with his other hand.

A good dribbler must also be able to change speed quickly. If he wants to accelerate to go past a defender, he must lean forward. This is called "leaning into the dribble." As he speeds past his opponent, the dribbler must control the ball from his waist to his chest. The speed dribble is a slightly higher dribble than normal.

There are other more advanced "moves" that you will want to practice. One is to change hands on the dribble by completely turning your back to an opponent. If you are coming at an opponent while dribbling with your right hand, watch him closely. If he seems to be heading for the ball, you can turn to the right quickly. As you do, pick the ball up with your left hand as you make the turn. Then complete the turn so your back is to your opponent and come out of it dribbling to the left with the left hand. Done quickly, this reverse dribble can be a tough move to stop.

Changing hands by swinging the ball behind the back is another eye-catching move. It can also be an effective one. But it takes practice. In this maneuver, instead of changing hands by bouncing the ball across your body, you will bounce it behind. Long arms help. It may also help at first to bend at the knees, into nearly a sitting position. Then try to bounce the ball close

A good dribbler will be able to change directions and switch hands quickly. One way to do this is to turn your back to the defender while dribbling slowly toward him. Look one way and maybe even take a quick "stutter-step," as if you are going to explode in that direction.

behind your heels as you can. The ball should come up just behind your left hip, where you can easily reach back with the left hand to get it. Then you can begin moving left.

All of these dribbling maneuvers take practice. Each coach will have different ball-handling drills for all his players. He may have you practice dribbling while on your knees and with your eyes closed. Or he might put a number of chairs or other objects on the floor and have his players weave in and out, back

If the defender leans in the direction of the fake, you can suddenly whirl the other way, switch the ball to your opposite hand, and burst past him. In all moves of this kind, the ballhandler must make his initial move very quickly. He must get past the defender and still maintain control of the dribble.

Another move that most young players learn today is the behind-the-back dribble. This can be done while moving downcourt or while being guarded closely by a defender. The ballhandler begins to move slowly toward the defender. He may fake right with a movement of his head or even by dipping his right shoulder.

He then starts his move by stepping forward with the foot opposite the hand controlling the ball. In this case, the left foot. At the same time, he swings the ball behind his back, ready to bounce it on the floor.

The bounce should be made at an angle that will bring the ball forward after it hits the floor. So the right hand must be a good distance behind the back at the release.

He can then reach behind with the left hand and pick up the ball. At the same time, he takes his first step with his back leg, now opposite the ball. He immediately goes into his dribble and begins to move past the player guarding him. The entire move must be made in a quick, smooth motion.

A good ballhandler will be able to do many things. To get around an opponent, it is often necessary to fake one way, then go hard the other way. Players often use this move when planning to drive to the hoop. To begin, the player pumps her arms to the right, as if she is going to dribble in that direction. She is trying to get the defender to lean the wrong way.

Once the defender takes the fake, the ballhandler quickly pulls the ball back across her body. At the same time, she takes a first, big step with her back foot.

She then picks up her pivot foot for the second step of the move. At the same time, she begins her dribble with the left hand. The defender has taken the fake just enough so that she is a split second late in reacting to the move.

Going hard to her left, the offensive player moves past the defender. Notice how she protects the dribble with her body. If the defender goes after the ball, she is likely to commit a foul.

31

and forth. Any drill that allows players to change hands and direction will make them better dribblers.

As you begin to play the game, you'll learn to protect the ball with you body and by dribbling away from your opponents. Keeping the ball in the right place will become second nature. You'll hardly have to look at the ball at all. It will be part of you.

Learning How To Pass

While dribbling is an important skill, it is something that should only be used when necessary. A player who dribbles too much is going to slow his team's attack. For dribbling is not the fastest way to move a basketball. The skill that means the most in a good offense is passing.

Skillful passing is the trademark of every good team. Even in the old days of the game, players whipped the ball around at eye-blink speed. That kind of passing not only keeps the defense off-balance, but often frees players for open shots. So every young person learning how to play the game of basketball must learn to pass. That means knowing the various kinds of passes and when to use them.

Before explaining the basic passes, one quick word. While every player must know how to pass, he must also know how to catch a pass. This should be done with both hands whenever possible. If the ball is above the waist, place the palms of your hands toward the ball, fingers up. Then spread the fingers, thumbs behind and almost touching. Your thumbs will keep the ball from slipping through your hands.

To catch a low pass below the waist, point the fingers down toward the floor with the palms again facing the ball. This time the little fingers will almost touch and make sure the ball doesn't slip through. Always watch the ball, right until you have it in your hands.

Another tip. Upon receiving the ball, protect it. Don't just hold it out in front where an opponent can slap it away or tie you up for a jump ball. Draw the ball in close to you. Or pivot around to protect it with your body. If you're tall, hold it up over your head, instead of at your waist.

But back to passing. There are four basic types of passes every young player must know. They are the *chest pass*, the *bounce pass*, the *baseball pass* and the *overhead pass*. Each has a purpose and a place where it should be used.

The chest pass, or two-hand chest pass, is perhaps the most common. It can be used in a number of court situations. A player with strong wrists can snap the pass off at great speed.

Left. The two-hand chest pass is the most basic pass in basketball. It begins with the ball being held close to the chest, thumbs behind the ball and almost touching. As the player prepares to make the pass, she should step directly toward her target. *Right.* The ball is delivered by pushing it away from the body while straightening the arms. A final, sharp snap of the wrist is what gives the pass its power.

To throw the chest pass, you should grip the ball with both hands, one on each side. The fingers should be spread wide apart with the thumbs directly behind the ball, almost touching each other. The pass will be thrown from chest level.

Always take a step toward your teammate as you throw the pass. This will help you get more power. As you step forward, push the ball away from your body, straightening your arms. A final snap of the wrists will give the pass its power and zing. Be sure to keep your elbows in close to your body. When you follow through, extend your arms, palms outward, and point your fingers toward your target.

A good chest pass can be used for short and medium ranges, and some stronger players will also use it for longer distances. It's still the most basic pass in basketball.

A bounce pass can sometimes catch the defense by surprise. It is also harder to intercept because of the time it takes for tall players to bend down for the ball. The ball is delivered from waist level. The pass can be made with one or two hands. If it is made with two hands, the chest pass motion is used. If it is made with one hand, the player should spread his fingers and keep his hand on top and to the side of the ball. A snap of the wrist gives the pass its power. It should bounce half to three-quarters of the way between the passer and target and be caught at waist level.

Next is the bounce pass, which is especially useful when there is a chance a chest pass might be intercepted. The pass is thrown just the way it sounds. The ball is bounced once on the floor and should come up right into the hands of the receiver.

The same basic technique is used as with the chest pass, except that the ball is thrown from about waist level. It is sometimes a good idea to bend down at the knees to better see the passing lane. The bounce should occur about halfway between passer and target, and that is the spot on the floor the passer must aim for. His follow through will be directed at that spot. Many people feel the bounce pass should hit the floor three-quarters of the way to the receiver. If the pass is thrown with backspin, it will bounce high and to the target.

A bounce pass, as a rule, is not as fast as a chest pass. So the passer should try to put some power in it and get rid of the ball quickly. One advantage of the pass is that it becomes a lot tougher for taller players to intercept, especially in traffic. The taller players just can't bend down fast enough to grab the ball.

The overhead pass is also thrown with two hands. Only the delivery is different. The pass is often used to throw the ball over the head of a defender. Thus it is thrown from up high.

Once again, the ball is held with fingers spread and the thumbs behind. The motion is similar to the chest pass. But the arm straightening and wrist snap are done from above the head. The passer again takes a step toward the target and follows through.

Power comes from the wrist snap. It won't help to bring the ball back behind your head for more power. All that will do is make the pass less accurate.

The fourth type of pass is the baseball pass. This is done just the way is sounds. The ball is thrown with one hand, with

Left. Another common pass thrown with two hands is the overhead pass. It is often used to toss the ball over the head of a defender. The passer begins by holding the ball high over his head with both hands. Once again, the fingers should be spread and thumbs held to the rear. As with the chest pass, the player takes a step toward his target before delivering the ball. *Right.* The pass is thrown by straightening the arms as they are brought forward. Once again, the power comes from a snap of the wrist. Don't make the mistake of bringing the ball back behind your head. That won't make the pass any stronger. But it will make it less accurate.

much the same motion a catcher uses to throw a baseball to second base. The pass is generally used to throw fast and long. Sometimes it is used after a rebound to reach another player who has broken downcourt ahead of the defenders.

The pass should come from right behind the ear. As with a

baseball throw, the passer should step into the throw, let his elbow come through first, then snap the ball with his wrist. On long passes, a player will find that by rolling the wrist inward (palm facing out), the ball will travel on a straight line and not curve.

Passes often have to be thrown quickly. Sometimes a player will fake a pass to one man before throwing to another. So a good passer will be able to see the entire floor, know where both his teammates and defenders are at all times. When he throws to a moving target, he should lead his man, much as a quarterback leads his wide receivers.

Another good fake is to look one way, while passing the other way. To do this well takes experience, because you are making almost a blind pass. But if you know where your man is and the distance, you can do it.

There are a number of other passes that more experienced players can use. Some players can pass right off the dribble, using one hand. Instead of pushing the ball back to the floor as it comes up, the dribbler will bring his hand up and either bounce or throw the ball through the air to a teammate.

One of the most exciting passes in basketball is the behind-the-back pass. This is also often done off the dribble. As the passer gets the ball on the bounce, he simply cradles it in his hand and flips it behind his back to a teammate. Throwing a perfect, behind-the-back pass on a fast break is one of the most spectacular plays in the game.

But beginners should still work on the fundamentals of the four basic passes. Here are some general tips on when to use each. The chest pass is the basic pass for the majority of situations. It is especially useful away from the basket, when a player is passing the ball from the point out front to the wing position.

The bounce pass is often used to get the ball inside, where the taller defenders will have trouble handling it. The baseball pass is used for long distances, while the overhead pass is mainly used to lob the ball over the head of a defender, especially a shorter one. It is also used as an *outlet pass* following a rebound.

As with dribbling, most coaches will have their teams working on different kinds of passing drills. Some involve just throwing the ball back and forth very rapidly. This strengthens the wrists and also the coordination. It also gives players a chance to catch as well as to pass.

Other drills might have the players hit moving targets, like a player cutting into the middle or running upcourt on a fast break. The player who is to receive the pass should also give the passer a target. He often does this by holding one hand up in the air as he makes his move.

Some basic rules for good passing are as follows. A passer should always look inside first. There might be a teammate open underneath the boards who can get a good, close-in shot. Another good rule is to pass into a space where a player is moving. That way, you aren't passing into heavy traffic where defenders can also move to get the ball. And last, always try to pass away from the defender, both the man guarding you and the one guarding your target.

This isn't always easy. But a good passing game is not easy, either. It takes work, practice, and coordination among team-mates. One or two players cannot do it alone. Even the greatest passer in the world won't get the job done, if he doesn't have open men to whom to pass.

So while you can practice alone against a wall, and maybe with a teammate, you must also practice passing with the entire team. As with all other parts of the game, a passer will only be successful through teamwork.

Learning How To Shoot

It is natural for every basketball player to want to shoot the ball. Many feel shooting is the most fun of all. It's certainly a great feeling to take a long, high arching shot and watch it swish through the hoop. But even so, a player who becomes shot happy, is going to hurt his team more than help it.

Still, it is important for every basketball player to know how to shoot. For it is the team with the most points that wins the game, and someone has to score those points. In fact, you never know when you'll suddenly get the ball and have to take the big shot with the game on the line. No one can make them all, but if you know the right way to shoot, you'll have a much better chance of being successful.

There are four kinds of shots—the *lay-up*, the *set* (or *push*) *shot*, the *jump shot*, and the *hook*. You may not get to use all four in a game, but it's still good to know how to shoot them.

Shooting a basketball has changed over the years. In the early days of the game, players often took long, two-handed set shots. In fact, with the exception of the lay-up, all shooting was done with two hands for many years. It wasn't until the 1930s that some players began to shoot one-handed, and it was still a decade or so before players began taking jump shots.

The jump shot has really changed the game. Today, most players can shoot the jump shot from anywhere on the floor. And because they can take it quickly and often jump above the defender, there is very little need for the standing set shot. But it is still a good idea to know how to make all the shots.

The easiest shot to make is the lay-up. That's because it is

Left. In order to protect the ball, a player can also shoot a short hook while almost facing the basket. The player here is in a position to shoot a regular lay-up. Instead, he is swinging his arm in the longer arc of the hook shot. If there were a defensive player in front of him, the hook would be much more difficult to block than the lay-up. *Right.* In shooting the basic lay-up, the player approaches the hoop from an angle. He should keep his head up and his eyes on the backboard. The jump comes off the leg opposite the shooting hand. The front leg is used to help propel the player upward. The other hand supports the ball until it is at face level. The player then continues toward the hoop with just the shooting hand on the ball. From both the right and left sides, the ball is always banked, or bounced, off the backboard above the rim. It should then drop back through the basket.

taken right under the basket. A shot from close in is called a "high percentage shot." The only shot with a higher percentage than a layup is a *dunk*. But not many young players are tall enough to dunk. That will come later.

Even though a lay-up is taken from in close, it is still important to know the right way to shoot it. That's because the player will sometimes be moving quickly as he goes in for the shot.

The lay-up is taken with one hand. When approaching from the right or left side of the basket, the player puts the ball up against the backboard and banks it into the basket. When the shooter approaches from right in front of the hoop, the ball is generally pushed over the front rim and in. However, younger players will have a better chance to make the shot if they veer to the left or right and use the backboard.

A shooter going in for a lay-up from the right side will jump off his left foot and shoot with his right hand. Going in from the left side, he will do it the opposite way. Players should be able to shoot their lay-ups with either hand.

To begin practicing the lay-up, a player can stand under the basket just off to one side. If he's on the right side, he'll push the ball with his right hand up toward the backboard. At the same time, he should push off his left leg, lifting his right knee up toward his waist. He should aim for a point on the backboard above and to the right of the basket. The ball should hit the backboard on the way up, glance lightly off it, then fall back through the basket.

Always watch the spot on the backboard where you want to put the ball. As you practice, you can begin to jump off your left foot more. Once you feel comfortable making the shot, you can start doing it by taking a two steps. The first is with the right foot, then the left, or takeoff, foot. Develop the ability to put a lot of power into the takeoff foot. On a lay-up, you'll want to go as high in the air as you can.

Once you begin to feel good taking the two steps, then you can begin shooting a real lay-up. That means dribbling to the hoop, taking a step with the right foot and exploding off the left foot. As you come off your last dribble, grab the ball with both hands and guide it to a point just above your head. Then let go with the non-shooting hand and complete the shot. This, of course, should be practiced from both sides of the basket and with both hands.

As with any kind of shot, concentration is very important. In a game, defensive players will try to stop the shooter in many ways. They may jump with him, bump him slightly, or even scream at him. Even if a player bumps you and is called for a foul, it's still important to make that shot. Because if you've already started to shoot before the foul was committed, the basket will count and you'll get a free throw on top of it.

The jump shot has become the most popular shot in basketball. Almost every player today, boy or girl, man or woman, develops a jump shot after playing for a while. There are a number of different styles of shooting, but every young player should learn some basic principles.

As with other shots, the player should begin shooting the jump shot fairly close to the basket. To shoot from far out too soon will cause him to force shots and develop bad habits. Getting the right form is more important. Distance, or range, will come later.

It is wise to begin no further than 10 feet from the basket. The jump should always be straight up, with the feet even and shoulder width apart. In fact, the shooter should come down on the same spot from which he jumped or slightly forward. The other thing young players ought to remember is that the

Left. The most popular shot in basketball today is the jump shot. A player should use the same form and technique for the shot from everywhere on the court. He must also shoot the same way, whether it is a standing jumper or a jump shot off the dribble. He should begin by squaring his body to the basket, no matter where he is on the court. As he gets ready to take the shot, he grabs the ball with both hands and crouches at the knees. The player shown here is just coming out of the crouch and starting to jump. he will spring off the soles of his feet, raising the ball over his head. His non-shooting hand will continue to guide the ball. *Center.* The player must take the shot at the very top of his jump. Once the ball is in shooting position, the player removes the guide hand. He should release the ball with his eyes focused firmly on the rim. The shooting motion involves straightening the arm and then smoothly flexing the wrist to follow through. The motion is similar to the push shot. *Right.* In the early days of basketball, the players all shot with two hands. Many could shoot a long, two-hand set shot from well behind the foul circle, launching the ball from high over their heads. It was an exciting shot to watch, but it is rarely used today.

43

shot itself should be taken at the top of the jump. If a player is sloppy and shoots on the way up or on the way down, his shot will not be as accurate.

The shooter, of course, cannot simply aim at the basket in general and hope the ball goes in. As a rule, he should try to put the ball in the basket just over the front rim or in front of the back rim. That's the target area on most shots, other than the lay-up. Either way, he must be consistent and always aim at the same spot.

Though there are some basic rules to follow, young shooters must develop their own sense of "touch." This is the way the ball feels in your hand, the way you release it, it's flight to the basket, and how it reacts when it hits the rim. The ball does not come off the rim hard if the shooter has a soft touch. There is more of a chance that the ball will bounce around and drop in.

Before going up for the jump shot, the shooter's body should be square to the basket. As he jumps in the air, he should use the following technique. The shooting hand should be behind the ball, fingers spread. The non-shooting hand is always placed on the side of the ball for extra support. The elbow should be under the ball and never sticking out at an angle to the body. Then the wrist should be cocked backwards, as if the shooter were carrying a flat object, such as a tray.

With the eyes always on the target, the shooter releases the shot at the top of the jump. The shot is made by straightening the arm at the elbow, then snapping the wrist forward. The ball should roll off the middle and index fingers last, and should have the backward spin that helps give it the "touch" described before. The follow through is very important. The shooter should make sure that the wrist is all the way forward and hold the arm steady for a second after the ball is released. To break from the shot motion too soon could affect the flight of the ball.

Left. It helps to be able to shoot with both hands in close to the basket. Shooting in close from the left side, the player goes off her right foot as she swings the ball up toward the hoop with a short, turnaround shot. Always make sure your palm is facing the backboard when you take the shot. *Right.* The technique from this point is the same as the lay-up. The player drives upward off her right foot and will bank the ball off the backboard and into the hoop.

There is a great deal more than technique that must be practiced with the jump shot. Once a young player has learned the technique and feels good about his shot, he can begin to increase his range. He will do this by simply practicing the shot from farther and farther away from the hoop. But he also has to get used to shooting in different situations.

A good offensive rebounder is always a big help to his team. It's not easy to rebound a teammate's shot. The defense often gets the best position. But a good offensive rebounder may be able to slip inside, get the ball, and put it right back into the basket.

For one thing, almost all jump shots will be taken with a defender very close to the shooter. The defender may jump with the shooter and try to block the shot. Even if he doesn't block it, he may break the shooter's concentration. So the player with the ball must be able to take his shot, no matter how close a defender is. Of course, if the defender hits the shooter's hand, arm, or any part of his body, he has committed a foul.

The shooter must also learn to take a jump shot off his dribble a split second after receiving a pass. This takes quickness and sure hands to control the ball. In shooting off a pass, the player must stop the second he receives the pass and be in the air before the defenders can react. Shooting off his own dribble, he must have the quickness to stop short and get up in the air in a smooth motion. Once the shooter is in the air, the technique for the shot remains the same.

There may be slight differences in the way each player shoots his jump shot. The important thing is to do it the same way each time. If his technique changes or varies, he cannot hope to be accurate.

To some, the set shot is part of basketball's past. There was a time when a player would hold the ball with both hands, and with a flick of his wrists, send long, two-handed set shots flying at the basket. But the jump shot helped to change all that.

However, the are still some players who will use the one-hand set, or push shot, at times. The shot is used mainly when a player is nearly unguarded. With no defensive pressure, the shooter can set himself and shoot without leaving the floor. The shooting motion for the one-hand push shot is identical to the jump shot. The fact that the shooter doesn't have to leave the floor cuts down on things that can go wrong.

When shooting the push shot, the player should place his feet about shoulder width apart. The right-handed shooter will have his right foot slightly in front of the left. His body should be square to the basket, the knees slightly bent. When he is ready to shoot, he will bring the ball up over his head, much as he did with the jump shot. The shooting motion and follow through are the same.

The difference is that the legs are also used in the shot. As the player begins the shooting motion, his legs straighten. At the point of the follow through, the shooter is up on his toes. Some even leave their feet slightly. The help from the legs gives the set shooter longer range and can even help him shoot better. It is a shot that uses the entire body.

In contrast, the hook shot is usually made in the middle of heavy traffic. Even so, it is very difficult to stop. That's because the shot is taken high over the head as the shooter turns sideways to the basket. His body is between the ball and the

The hook shot is usually taken by a big man in close to the basket. A righthanded shooter will usually begin with his back to the basket. The shot is made with a long, upward sweep of the arm. The player will pivot on his opposite foot so he is sideways to the hoop. As he swings the ball up past shoulder level, he rises on the toes of his opposite foot. He then releases the ball with a flick of the wrist as his arm reaches its highest point.

defender. Since hook shots are usually taken by big men, that makes them even harder to stop.

But a hook shot isn't for everyone, especially not beginners. It is not as easy to control as a jump shot or push shot. Because of the long, circular sweep of the arm, a large hand is helpful in controlling the ball. That's why young players will have trouble developing this shot.

When the shooter is ready to hook, he will stride forward with his left foot. He is now sideways to the basket, and begins the upward sweep with his right arm. Rising up on the toes of his left foot and bringing his right knee up, the shooter continues the upward arc of his arm. He releases the ball at the

Left. **Most players shoot their free throws with the same motion as the jump shot. It is essentially a push shot. A player must learn to relax on the foul line, bounce the ball a few times, and take a deep breath. Then he should bring the ball up over his head, using the non-shooting hand as a guide. he should also bend slightly at the knees before shooting.** *Right.* **The shot is taken by straightening the arm and letting the ball roll off the fingertips. Many players get a little extra push from their legs and end up on their toes when they follow through. Remember to keep your eyes on the basket and aim the ball just over the front rim.**

highest point of the arc. Then he flicks his wrist and lets the ball roll off his fingertips with a backward rotation.

It takes a good deal of practice to shoot the hook shot well. But even then, it is not a shot that can be used very often during a game. So it should be practiced only after the others have been learned.

Another word about shooting. There comes a time when all players must take foul shots. These are free shots from behind the foul line, fifteen feet from the basket. The player will be unguarded and unhurried, so he should make a very high percentage of free throws. But when he stands on the line during the heat of a game, there is a great deal of pressure to make the shot. That doesn't help.

The first thing a player on the foul line should do is relax. This is important. The shooter cannot be tense. He should bounce the ball a few times, concentrating on the basket. Then just before shooting, he should take a deep breath. Most players today take a one-hand push shot from the foul line. The technique is the same as described earlier. The key is to relax, concentrate, and follow through. And, of course, practice. Most coaches will end all practice sessions by having everyone shoot free throws, maybe fifty or more. Many games have been both won and lost from the foul line.

There is no substitute for good shooting. A poor-shooting team will have trouble winning games. So it is vital for every team and every player to work hard on their shots. Of course, the complete player will do everything well. That's what all players must strive for.

Learning How To Rebound

Since every shot does not go into the basket, those that are missed are up for grabs. A missed shot becomes a rebound. And rebounding is another important part of the sport. If the team on defense gets the rebound, they can move downcourt and go on offense. But if a member of the offensive team gets the rebound, he can put it right back into the basket. Or he can pass the ball back to a teammate and keep his team on offense.

Besides good position, rebounding takes strength and toughness. When you get the ball with several players around you, hold on tight. Protect the ball either by keeping it high over your head or by spreading your elbows out to the sides. Then try to pass or dribble out of trouble.

As a general rule, the biggest, tallest players are the best rebounders. But there are some tricks that every player can learn that will make him a better rebounder.

Rebounding isn't easy. The battle under the boards can get rough. While basketball isn't a contact sport, every player going for a rebound is going to be bumped and pushed at some time or other.

Timing and position play a great role in good rebounding. So does desire. Sometimes the player who is willing to fight the

Good rebounding is a big help to a basketball team. The best rebounders jump well, have a good sense of timing and really want the ball. Even if you think you are alone underneath the basket, go hard for the ball. Get positioned, jump high, grab the ball with both hands and protect it. Then try to make a quick pass to a teammate.

hardest for the ball is the one who will get it. Let's take a look at each of these elements, one by one.

A player going for a rebound has to jump as high as he possibly can. That's because other players are going to be jumping as well. To have a chance for the ball, he must time his moves so that he will reach the ball at the very top of his jump. Since he will grab the rebound with his arms extended high over his head, he will be at the highest position he can be.

This takes practice, as a missed shot doesn't come off the rim the same way twice. So the rebounder must watch the flight of the ball carefully. When he sees it hit the rim, he must judge quickly how and when it will come down. Then he must make a strong and decisive move to get that basketball. If he times his jump badly, he will have no chance to get the rebound.

Of course, a player can have the best timing in the world and it won't help him much if he doesn't get "position." That means being in the right spot to go after the rebound. As soon as the shot is on its way up, the rebounder tries to get to the spot where he thinks the ball will come off. He has to move quickly and try to slide or cut in front of opposing rebounders. But he cannot push them out of the way. That could mean a violation.

Once the rebounder has position, he must try to prevent his opponents from getting inside him. He does this by "boxing out." That means getting low, feet and arms spread wide, and actually blocking the path to the basket for the opponent. Once the player has position, an opponent behind him cannot push

Boxing out is a big part of rebounding. Once the rebounder gets position underneath, he must protect that position. That means spreading his feet and arms and getting down low. He is then ready to go for the ball. The players behind him cannot try to push him out of the way or they will foul. Their only hope of getting the rebound is to jump over him. And that, too, often leads to a foul.

53

or pull him. The opponent is boxed out, and the only chance he has is to jump over the other player.

Defensive players will often try to box out opponents after a shot to keep them away from the boards. Even the man guarding the shooter should try to block the path to the basket. That way, the shooter cannot follow his own shot for a possible offensive rebound.

Remember that once you have position, you've got to go hard for the basketball. Some players like to keep their legs spread apart after the jump. They feel it will help keep opponents away. Whenever possible, the rebound should be grabbed with two hands, and grabbed hard. For as soon as you come down, your opponents will try to take the ball away or tie you up.

If you are a tall rebounder, you can simply keep the ball high above your head when you come down. Then you can throw an overhead "outlet pass" to a teammate. Even if you don't hold the ball aloft, you should never bring it down low. That makes it easy prey. Bring the ball down to chin level, still holding it tight. You can also keep your elbows out, away from your body, to further protect the ball.

If an opponent is in front of you and going for the ball, pivot away from him and look for a teammate. If there is an open court, you can also dribble the ball out of traffic before passing.

As a rule, the defensive team is going to be closer to the board than the offensive players. That's why there are more defensive rebounds than offensive rebounds in a game. Offensive rebounding is a real skill. Players must be quick and aggressive to avoid being boxed out. Sometimes they can fake the defensive man by pretending to go one way, then go the other and slip inside.

If the ball comes down to the side of the basket and the offensive player feels he cannot grab it, he may try to tip the ball back in. This is done by pushing at the ball with one or two hands. The trick is to get enough of your hand on the ball to direct it back into the hoop. Again, this is something that takes practice.

Every coach knows the value of a good rebounding team. In fact, some coaches even put a cover on top of the hoop so that every shot in practice becomes a rebound. The more rebounds a team gets, the better chance they have to win the game.

Learning To Play Defense

Most great teams in the history of basketball, especially the pro game, have been great defensive teams. More often than not, it's defense that makes the difference in the playoffs and championship games. And each player must be able to help in the defensive effort.

There are two basic styles of defense in basketball. They are the *zone defense* and the *man-to-man defense*. The zone defense is not allowed in professional basketball, but is allowed everywhere else and is quite popular.

The difference in the two types of defenses is simple. In a zone defense, each player covers a specific area of the court. He will guard any man who comes into that area. But he won't follow that man when he moves out of the area. Another defender will pick him up.

In a man-to-man defense, each player guards a specific opponent. Therefore, he will follow that man wherever he goes on the court. If, for some reason, he loses his man, then he must switch with another defender. He will take his teammate's man so his teammate can cover for him. But the players usually switch back as soon as they can.

Defense is based on quickness and hustle. If you work very hard for the entire game, you will usually produce good results.

In a zone defense, each player must cover a certain area of the court. All players should be in the defensive stance, arms up, ready to go into action as the offense comes at them. There are several different types of zones. Each coach will make his own choice, depending on the players he has.

To begin with, you must know the basic defensive stance.

Start with your feet comfortably apart, at least shoulder width, with one foot a little in front of the other. Your hands should be low and out to the side, palms out and fingers spread. Bend at the knees and keep a low center of gravity. Your weight should be on the balls of your feet so you can move quickly in any direction.

It may be tempting to lean forward from this position. But you should not fall into this trap. Defenders often find themselves moving backward, so they should keep their weight centered, even slightly back. The position may seem a bit awkward at first, but you will soon get used to it.

Keeping the hands up and moving has been a defensive basketball rule for years. In a zone defense, all players should keep their arms up and waving, except the one playing the ball. That will tend to make it tougher for the offense to pass and will make an interception more likely. The man playing the ball, of course, should take the normal defensive stance (shown below).

You should always play the man with the ball very tightly. Stay close to him, move your hands, and try to force him out of his game. If you make it easy for him to dribble past you, pass into the middle, or even move in close with the ball, then you haven't done your job. If your opponent is a good ballhandler, he can pick out an open man for an easy basket.

Defenders must also work together. That means talking constantly, telling your teammate what is going on behind him. Sometimes the offense will try to "pick a defender off." That means an offensive player will come out and stand his ground at a certain spot on the court. He is setting the "pick."

The player at the right is using the basic, defensive stance. With feet spread apart, one in front of the other, and knees bent, he can move quickly in every direction. He should also keep his hands out to the side, ready to play the ball or intercept a pass.

His teammate, usually the man with the ball, will then dribble right past his unmoving teammate. If the defensive man doesn't see the pick, he will run right into it. That means he will not only lose his man, but he may commit a foul as well.

Most defensive players will move from side to side with a shuffle step. That's where quickness comes in. The steps are short and quick. The feet do not cross over one another. That way, the defender is never out of position, and almost always in the defensive stance ready to change direction. If the man you're guarding starts to shoot, you can quickly move up and either try to block the shot or distract him.

It takes a great deal more energy to play man-to-man defense than it does zone. Teams that play a man-to-man defense have to be in very good physical condition. All the players are moving constantly, on both offense and defense. Yet a smooth-working zone defense can really put a blanket on an offense as well.

One special kind of man-to-man defense is the *full court press*. A team that presses picks up their opponents as soon as the ball comes in bounds. Normally, the defense waits for the offense in the frontcourt. But with the press, they begin in the backcourt and guard their men closely all over. They try to disrupt the dribbler or intercept passes. In other words, they do everything to prevent the offense from setting up and trying for the good shot.

Defense takes hard work. It's as simple as that. Work and desire can help make anyone a good defensive player. A young person who thinks he can relax on defense just because he is a good scorer on offense will not be a good basketball player. For basketball is a team game, and that means playing hard at both ends of the court.

Some Offensive Tips

Each coach has his own ideas about offense. Some will want their players to run and fast break whenever they have a chance. Others prefer a half-court offense. That is, bringing the ball into the frontcourt, then running the offense. Often the types of players a coach has will tell him what kind of offense is best for the team.

Some teams will simply freelance. The players know each other so well that they cut and move, set picks and screens, and just keep moving to get free. Others have set patterns for the players to run on offense. A weave, for instance, involves constant movement of all the players. They take turns cutting down the middle, then looping through the frontcourt and into the backcourt again.

Still other offenses work off the center—the big man in the middle. The other players will try to pass the ball inside to the big man, who stands just outside the free-throw lane near the basket (an offensive player cannot stay inside the lane for more than three seconds). Then they might cut past him for a possible return pass.

So there are all kinds of offensive patterns a team can use. In general, however, players must know how to move without the ball. That means you can't just stand around, waiting for a pass. The object of playing offense is to get free for a good shot. If you are being guarded by one man, you must fake and cut, always trying to lose him. Sometimes you can run him into a pick. Other times, you can fake one way, then move quickly in the other direction.

If you get open, there is a good chance a teammate will spot you and get the ball to you. Then you can try to dribble, or drive to the hoop for a lay-up. Or you can try a quick jump shot. You always look for the best shot. And the better ones always come from in close.

Movement also helps against a zone defense. Even though one man isn't guarding you, faking and moving can confuse all the defensive players in the zone. Or you can manage to slip inside one of the seams in the zone and get open that way. So no matter what kind of defense you run into, constant movement is a good way to deal with it. A player who moves well without the ball has the best chance of getting open for a shot or even being fouled.

All offensive players should also know how to set and use picks. If a teammate has the ball at the top of the key (the name for the foul lane and circle around the foul line), you can come out and set up perhaps 10 or 15 feet to his right. Then stand there, legs shoulder-width apart, hands at your side. If your teammate wants to use the pick, he will begin dribbling toward you.

Don't move, even if the defender is going to run into you. The next step is up to your teammate with the ball. He should dribble very close to your shoulder if he wants to pick his man off. If he leaves too much room, the defender can fight through the pick and continue to guard the man with the ball. But if the defender runs into the pick, the ballhandler is open to drive to the hoop or pass. If the defender goes behind the pick (behind you), the ballhandler can pull up and take a jump shot.

So picks and screens are a valuable part of an offense. All players should know how to set and use them. A pick can also become a different kind of offensive weapon when it is part of a "pick and roll." Here, the player setting the pick waits for the ball handler to move past him. If he catches the defense switching assignments or napping, he can suddenly whirl or roll and cut quickly to the basket. He is hoping for a quick pass from the ballhandler for an easy hoop.

A variation of the pick and roll is the "give and go." Two players can work this very well. The player with the ball passes it to a teammate, then makes a quick move to the basket. He is trying to get the ball passed right back for a lay-up. Longtime teammates have a kind of sixth sense on a give and go. Or they can signal each other with a quick glance or nod of the head. Again, it depends on quickness and catching the defense by surprise.

The object of basketball may be simple, but the game is not. There are many ways for an offense to attack a defense, and many ways for the defense to stop the offense. All of it comes down to a team, playing together and playing hard. Yet the

A good, crisp passing game is an important part of every offense. Players move and cut, and the man with the ball has to be ready to deliver a quick pass that might lead to a basket. Here, an offensive player starts to cut down the middle between two defenders. The man with the ball is getting set for a quick chest pass.

team is made up of individuals. And the individuals must know all the fundamentals of the game—dribbling, passing, shooting, rebounding, and defensive play.

So you must start with the fundamentals and practice them over and over again. Do not take any one part of the game for granted. You may be a great scorer, but if you don't play defense well, you will hurt your team. You may be a great passer, but if you can't put the ball on the floor and dribble, you will hurt your team. You may play excellent defense, but if you can't make a simple lay-up, sooner or later you will hurt your team.

The whole of basketball is made up of all the parts. When all the parts are working, a team becomes great. Every young player must work to become the best player he can possibly be. Then, if he becomes part of a team, he can do the job.

It's high fives all around when a team wins the big game or the championship. And it can happen if all the players take time to learn the fundamentals of basketball. Then it takes practice and a good coach to put it all together.

Glossary

Backboard The 4′×6′ rectangular board on which the basket is suspended. There is also a smaller, half-moon backboard used for outdoor and backyard courts.

Backcourt Name given to the half of the court that a team is defending. The backcourt at any given time depends on which team has the ball.

Baseball Pass A pass thrown with one hand. The motion is almost identical to that of a catcher throwing a baseball.

Bounce Pass Pass in which the ball is bounced once midway between the passer and the receiver.

Boxing Out Term used to describe one player blocking another from getting good position underneath the boards for a rebound.

Center Usually a tall player who plays close to the basket in the middle of the offense. He is also likely to play underneath on defense. He should be a good rebounder.

Chest Pass The most basic basketball pass. It is made with two hands from chest level. Both the arms and wrists are used to snap the ball to a teammate.

Dribbling Moving the basketball up or down the court by bouncing it with either hand.

Fast Break Moving the ball upcourt as fast as possible after a rebound in an effort to catch the defensive team napping. If done right, a fast break can lead to an easy basket.

Field Goal Name given to a successful shot from anywhere on the court, with the exception of a free throw.

Forwards The two players who play alongside the center on offense. They are part of the team's front line. Forwards usually play in the forecourt near the corners and end line. They tend to be tall.

Foul Lane A 12 or 16-foot area that extends from the end line to the free throw line on both ends of the court. Offensive players cannot stay in the lane for more than three seconds at a time.

Fouling Out Refers to a player being forced to leave the game for committing the maximum number of personal fouls allowed. It is usually five or six.

Foul Line Line drawn on the court 15 feet from the back. Free throws must be shot from behind this line.

Free Throw Also called a foul shot. This is an unhindered shot at the basket after a foul has been committed. Players get one or two shots, depending on the foul and also the number of team fouls. A free throw counts as one point.

Frontcourt The offensive half of the basketball court. The frontcourt is whichever end the offensive team happens to be in at any time.

Give and Go An offensive play in which a player makes a pass and cuts to the basket for a quick return pass.

Goal Tending Deflecting a shot that is already on its downward path to the

63

basket. This is a violation. Even if the deflected shot doesn't go in, the basket still counts.

Guards   Two players who usually do most of the ballhandling and play farthest away from the basket on offense. Guards are generally not as tall as forwards and the center.

Hook Shot   Type of shot usually taken by a big man in close. The player turns sideways to the basket and swings his shooting arm around in a wide arc, releasing the ball at the top of the arc.

Hoop   Nickname for the basket.

Jump Shot or Jumper   The most popular shot in basketball today. It is released from above the head when the shooter is at the top of his jump.

Key   Traditional name for the free-throw lane and circle. In the old days of the game, the lane was just six feet wide and was actually the shape of a key.

Lay-Up   Basic shot made from underneath the basket. The ball is usually banked off the backboard before it drops through the net.

Man-to-Man Defense   Popular defense in which each defensive player guards a particular man, instead of an area.

Outlet Pass   Name given to a quick pass made after a defensive rebound. It is usually intended to start a fast break.

Overhead Pass   Two-handed style of passing in which the ball is held, then released from a position over the passer's head.

Pick and Roll   Play in which a player setting a pick suddenly rolls to the basket for a quick return pass.

Pick or Screen   A legal blocking maneuver in which an offensive player sets up in a spot where a defensive player will have to pass to cover his man.

Pivot   Term used for the area close to the basket where the center generally plays. It also describes a maneuver by a player who turns away from an opponent by moving one foot while keeping the second, or pivot foot, on the floor.

Rebound   Any missed shot that hits the backboard or rim and "rebounds" back toward the floor.

Set Shot   A shot taken with one or two hands while both feet remain on the floor.

Switch   What happens when two defensive players temporarily change their guarding assignments during the flow of the game.

Traveling   A violation called when a player takes too many steps without dribbling the ball. The penalty is loss of the ball for the team.

Weave   Offensive formation in which all the players run a set pattern over and over again on the court.

Zone Defense   Popular type of defense in which each player covers a set area of the court, instead of a particular man.